THE **I AM** JOURNAL

THE **I AM** JOURNAL

Created by Lauren Sanders

Published by Think and Ink Company

ISBN: 978-0-692-92173-9

© Think and Ink Company LLC. All rights reserved.

Book design by Vanessa Maynard

Get in touch

hello@thinkandinkco.com

THE I AM JOURNAL

www.thinkandinkco.com

"The greater danger is not that our hopes are too high and we fail to reach them, it's that they are too low and we do."

MICHELANGELO

YOU ARE AMAZING.

Everything you need to create the life of your dreams is already within you. But to unleash this greatness, you must be willing to change the way you think, feel and act.

With the right mindset, your success is limitless. Think of The I AM Journal as your own personal coach, training you to develop a powerful mindset that becomes stronger each day. By following these simple daily rituals, you can radically transform your life.

The I AM Journal puts the Law of Attraction into action, helping you spiritually manifest your burning desires.

Be ambitious. Be aligned. Be amazing.

You can do this. Let's get started.

"By believing passionately in something that still does not exist, we create it. The nonexistent is whatever we have not sufficiently desired."

FRANZ KAFKA

Table of Contents

"If one advances confidently in the direction of their dreams, and endeavors to live the life which he has imagined, he will meet with a success unexpected in common hours."

HENRY DAVID THOREAU

THREE WAYS THE I AM
JOURNAL WILL HELP YOU

You will develop a mindset that will allow you to live your dream life. A mindset is not a set-it-and-forget-it type of thing. It's something that must be constantly nurtured to make your burning desires a reality. Shifting your mindset to one that believes all things are possible is the foundation to creating your best life. It requires accepting new truths about your limitless capabilities and casting aside your old ideas of what you can achieve. Only then can you break through the ceiling of limitations you've created for yourself and achieve your most burning desires.

Through gratitude, you will attract more to be grateful for in your life. By expressing appreciation for the wonderful things present in your daily life, you will send a positive energy into the universe. The more positive your energy, the more positive things you'll attract. In other words, like attracts like. Gratitude reduces negativity. The happier you are, the sooner you can create the mindset required to transform your desires into your reality.

Daily accountability means you're constantly taking the next steps to creating your best life.

Think of The I AM Journal as a personal trainer waiting for you at the gym every single day. We achieve our best results when we hold ourselves accountable. By investing 15 minutes in ourselves daily to work on our mindset and take intentional steps to achieve the success we are seeking, we become closer to manifesting our burning desires.

"I AM.
Two of the most
powerful words; for
what you put after
them shapes your
reality."

BEVAN LEE

THE POWER OF I **AM**

To illustrate the power of I AM, let's do this exercise. Compare how you feel after reading the following I AM statements.

I AM tired.	I AM love.
I AM sick.	I AM light.
I AM weak.	I AM grateful.
I AM poor.	I AM magnificent.
I AM unlucky.	I AM limitless.

Words have power. They affect how we feel. Our feelings impact how we think, act and even influence the energy we give to the universe. You get what you give to the universe.

If you repeat negative I AM affirmations, your feelings become in sync with these negative thoughts. Guess what happens if you spend time focusing on what you *don't* like about your life? You will continue to attract more of what you don't want.

Life will prove you right. If you come from a place of lack, the universe will respond in kind with a lack of abundance in your life. God does not come from a place of lack. He is abundant, and we were created in His image. Be aligned with our creator and what He intended for us.

FOUR TIPS FOR USING THE POWER OF I **AM**:

1. Don't focus on your current life circumstances. Focus on what you want to create for yourself. For example, if you want to attract financial abundance to your life, don't say, "I am tired of being poor." Instead, say "I am wealthy."

2. Remember, it's not "I will be." It's "I AM." Make your affirmations certain and in the present. For example, don't say, "I will be starting my own business one day." Instead of making future proclamations, say, "I am a successful entrepreneur."

3. If you find yourself thinking negative I AM affirmations, tell yourself, "Right now, I choose to stop limiting myself with these untrue beliefs." Don't be too hard on yourself or dwell in the matter. Focus on the present and begin saying your positive I AM affirmations.

4.　Repeat your I AM affirmations in your mind before bedtime to program your subconscious mind. Your subconscious mind influences your thoughts, feelings and behaviors – all of which shape your life. As Thomas Edison said, "Never go to sleep without a request to your subconscious."

"Thoughts become things. If you see it in your mind, you will hold it in your hand."

BOB PROCTOR

THREE LAW OF ATTRACTION PRINCIPLES

1. YOU GET WHAT YOU GIVE.

The more you give to the universe, the more you'll receive in return. Just like any other relationship you cherish, your relationship with the universe can't be one-sided. Ask the universe, "How may I serve you today?" If you focus on serving the higher good, the universe will reciprocate in kind by serving you.

Here are a few ways to accomplish this:

Meditate or pray for answers: This will put you in alignment with God and allow you to hear Him more clearly. Ask for guidance on how you can serve the highest good today, and you will receive clarity. Whether through images that manifest in your mind, your inner voice, or God's wisdom, you will receive answers. Through this connection with our divine creator, you'll feel more joyful, which releases a positive energy to the universe.

Be joyful: By choosing to feel joyful, your positive energy will spread to others. This activates a powerful domino effect throughout the universe. Your joyful presence makes others feel happy, which helps them to bring this same positive energy into their interactions with others. You have the power to positively impact how others choose to see the world.

Choose to see love: If you want to see wonderful things come into your life, then you must change the way you see life. Our creator, who gave us all life, is the source of love. By seeing the world through His eyes – with love – we intentionally bring more love to our emotional state. Choosing love drastically influences our energy with others, our words and our thoughts. In every situation, choose grace, compassion and empathy over negativity and judgment, and you'll give more positive energy to the universe every time.

2. ARE YOU FEELING IT?

The universe responds to your feelings. This is why it is crucial to, in Neville Goddard's words, "Assume the feeling of the wish fulfilled." By thinking as if your burning desire has already manifested itself in your life, the positive feelings you'll associate with living your dream life will come naturally to your present-day self. You will exude these feelings of joy to the universe, releasing a positive vibration that brings you closer to spiritually manifesting your burning desire.

Remember: like attracts like. By changing your emotional state to one that mirrors how you will feel when you attract your burning desire, the universe will match that energy and bring more of it into your life. Stay in alignment with the feeling of the wish fulfilled.

Take note of what environmental circumstances positively or negatively influence your emotional state. While it sounds simple, do more of what makes you happy and avoid what doesn't bring you joy. When you find yourself in situations that bring your energy down, do your best to choose to see things in a different, more positive way.

Your feelings play another crucial role in creating your best life. Instead of asking the universe only for *what* you want, be certain of how you want to *feel* when that burning desire becomes a reality. The universe responds to our feelings. This means that instead of thinking that you want to have a five-figure sales month for your business, think instead that you want to feel supported and valued by your customers.

Here's an exercise to help you make this mindset shift. First, write a list of what you want to attract:

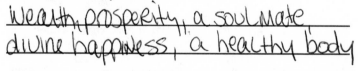

Wealth, prosperity, a soul mate divine happiness, a healthy body

Now, pick the one thing you want to attract more than anything. This is your burning desire. Write it down again below:

Wealth

Then, think about how you will feel when you attract it and complete this sentence below:

I want to feel

Free, happy, healthy, wealthy & wise

Whenever you find yourself focusing more on the outcome, stop and turn your focus on the above statement. Our feelings not only influence the vibrations we offer to the universe, they impact our experiences, how we see the world and how we make decisions. Feelings matter.

3. REMEMBER ALL THINGS ARE POSSIBLE.

For the law of attraction to work, you must trust in a higher power. We came from God. He is love. Through Him, all things are possible. If you doubt that your burning desire will come true, then you are doubting the powerful source that creates miracles in our lives.

You must believe. Easier said than done, right? When you find yourself losing faith in this journey, acknowledge it. Then choose a different way to feel. Find something in that moment to be grateful for and choose to feel that joy instead. As Wayne Dyer said, "If you change the way you look at things, the things you look at change." The signs are there, but it's up to you to recognize them.

God wants us to be love, spread love and feel loved through Him. By accepting this as our birthright and natural state of being, we can turn our backs to the doubt that will prevent us from realizing our burning desire.

Accept that you have the right to feel joyful and manifest anything you desire into your life. Only you can take this right away from yourself. God wants to give you everything you want. It's up to you to allow it to happen. Choose belief over doubt, and you will be amazed at what this decision will bring to your life.

"There is one quality which one must possess to win, and that is definiteness of purpose, the knowledge of what one wants, and a burning desire to possess it."

NAPOLEON HILL

HOW TO CREATE YOUR
BURNING DESIRE STATEMENT

Now that you have a better understanding of the role our feelings play in manifesting your ideal life, it's time to create your burning desire statement.

Think of your burning desire statement as your compass on this journey. Make sure your thoughts, feelings, affirmations and intentional actions are aligned with this statement. Daily repetition of your burning desire statement will keep you focused on what you are striving to achieve.

When thinking of what your burning desire is, remember two things:

1. Be limitless.

2. Focus on how it will make you feel.

On page 24, you conducted an exercise to discover how you wanted your burning desire to make you feel. You may have a different burning desire now than the one you identified on that page. That's okay. Trust your instinct on which burning desire would bring you the most joy in your life. For the intention of this journal, it's important to focus on manifesting one burning desire at a time and be very clear with the universe through this burning desire statement.

Complete the below sentence:

I have a burning desire to feel

Supported by the universe and help limitless amount of people with salt therapy at the Salt SPA.

Here's an example of a burning desire statement I created when I started to develop The I AM Journal:

"I have a burning desire to feel supported by the universe and help a limitless amount of people with The I AM Journal."

"*You can't just think and grow rich, you've got to do something with those thoughts.*"

BOB PROCTOR

HOW TO USE
THE I AM JOURNAL

To prime your mindset each day to manifest your ideal life, it's important to have a morning and evening journaling routine. Beginning your day with this morning ritual, especially in conjunction with prayer and meditation, is a powerful way to consciously guide your thoughts, feelings and actions for the remainder of the day.

At the conclusion of each day, the evening journaling routine will cultivate feelings of joy and accomplishment before you go to sleep. Before your head hits the pillow, you will have taken an integral step to program your subconscious mind and attract what you desire most for your life.

THE MORNING RITUAL EXPLAINED

Your burning desire statement:

Refer to page 28 for the burning desire statement you created. By recommitting it to paper daily, it'll serve as a constant guidepost of what you are manifesting into your life. Your thoughts, feelings, affirmations and actions should be in alignment with making your burning desire a reality.

What intentional actions will you take today to attract it?

From concrete action steps to reminding yourself to bring joy to every interaction with others, this list helps you consciously create and follow through with three daily actions that will influence your ability to manifest your burning desire.

How will you feel while making these conscious efforts?

As mentioned earlier, the universe responds to our feelings. This is why it's important to recognize how performing these intentional acts will make us feel. The more positive our feelings, the more positivity we'll attract to our lives.

I AM:

Through daily affirmations, you consciously reinforce what you want to feel, be and achieve. These are to be written in the present tense as though the transformation has already occurred. Include affirmations that begin with "I am feeling" too so that you can directly channel those feelings and release this positive energy.

By repeating your affirmations in the morning and evening, you'll set your intentions, feelings and vibrations for the day and program your subconscious before you fall asleep.

Wayne Dyer developed a powerful subconscious programming exercise he called "Now I lay me down to sleep." Repeat your I AM affirmations for five minutes in your mind after your head rests on the pillow. While you are repeating these, also assume the feeling of the wish fulfilled. Focus on feeling as though you are already living from this way of being – not aspiring to it. By falling asleep in the state of feeling as though your burning desire has already manifested itself into your life, it will retrain your subconscious mind to automatically think, feel and act on what you are manifesting.

THE EVENING RITUAL EXPLAINED

What three things are you grateful for today?

Practicing gratitude and recognizing the abundance of wonderful things that bring you great happiness are instrumental to your daily routine. By giving attention and appreciation to the things that spark joy in our lives, we release a tremendous amount of positive energy into the universe, which is an essential part of the law of attraction process.

How did you serve the universe today?

Our relationship with the universe can't be one-sided if we expect it to deliver an abundance of wonderful gifts into our lives. Recognize instances where you demonstrated kindness to others on a daily basis, and you'll be amazed how this positively impacts your mood.

How does it feel to experience your burning desire today?

Close your eyes and picture your life as if your burning desire is now a reality. Notice how this makes you feel, and let it flow on the page. By experiencing your burning desire in the present tense, you'll find it easier to be grateful, have faith and take the actions required to attract what you want. As Neville Goddard said, "So live in the feeling of being the one you want to be and you shall be."

"*Once you make
a decision, the
universe conspires
to make it happen.*"

RALPH WALDO EMERSON

THE **I AM** JOURNAL

MORNING RITUAL FOR __11__ / __5__ / __20__

Your burning desire statement:

I have the burning desire to be
supported by the universes and to
be a successful business woman today

What intentional actions will you take today to attract it?

1. - Reach out to others about my SPA
2. - Share the opportunity of touchstone Jewelry
3. - Be creative

How will you feel while making these conscious efforts?

Joyful, Happy

I AM:

Healthy wealthy and wise
I am love, I am light, I am
greatful, I am magnificent
I AM LIMItless!

EVENING RITUAL FOR ___ / ___ /___

I AM:

_____

_____

_____

What three things are you grateful for today?

1.

2.

3.

How did you serve the universe today?

_____

_____

_____

How does it feel to experience your burning desire today?

_____

_____

_____

MORNING RITUAL FOR ___ / ___ /___

Your burning desire statement:

_____

_____

_____

What intentional actions will you take today to attract it?

1.

2.

3.

How will you feel while making these conscious efforts?

_____

_____

_____

I AM:

_____

_____

_____

EVENING RITUAL FOR   __ / __ /__

I AM:

_____

_____

_____

What three things are you grateful for today?

1.

2.

3.

How did you serve the universe today?

_____

_____

_____

How does it feel to experience your burning desire today?

_____

_____

_____

MORNING RITUAL FOR   __ / __ /__

Your burning desire statement:

_____

_____

_____

What intentional actions will you take today to attract it?

1.

2.

3.

How will you feel while making these conscious efforts?

_____

_____

_____

I AM:

_____

_____

_____

EVENING RITUAL FOR ___ / ___ /___

I AM:

_____

_____

_____

What three things are you grateful for today?

1.

2.

3.

How did you serve the universe today?

_____

_____

_____

How does it feel to experience your burning desire today?

_____

_____

_____

MORNING RITUAL FOR ___ / ___ /___

Your burning desire statement:

_____

_____

_____

What intentional actions will you take today to attract it?

1.

2.

3.

How will you feel while making these conscious efforts?

_____

_____

_____

I AM:

_____

_____

_____

EVENING RITUAL FOR   ___ / ___ /___

I AM:

_____

_____

_____

What three things are you grateful for today?

1.

2.

3.

How did you serve the universe today?

_____

_____

_____

How does it feel to experience your burning desire today?

_____

_____

_____

MORNING RITUAL FOR ___ / ___ /___

Your burning desire statement:

_____

_____

_____

What intentional actions will you take today to attract it?

1.

2.

3.

How will you feel while making these conscious efforts?

_____

_____

_____

I AM:

_____

_____

_____

EVENING RITUAL FOR ___ / ___ /___

I AM:

_____

_____

_____

What three things are you grateful for today?

1.

2.

3.

How did you serve the universe today?

_____

_____

_____

How does it feel to experience your burning desire today?

_____

_____

_____

MORNING RITUAL FOR ___ / ___ /___

Your burning desire statement:

_____

_____

_____

What intentional actions will you take today to attract it?

1.

2.

3.

How will you feel while making these conscious efforts?

_____

_____

_____

I AM:

_____

_____

_____

EVENING RITUAL FOR ___ / ___ /___

I AM:

_____

_____

_____

What three things are you grateful for today?

1.

2.

3.

How did you serve the universe today?

_____

_____

_____

How does it feel to experience your burning desire today?

_____

_____

_____

MORNING RITUAL FOR ___ / ___ /___

Your burning desire statement:

_____

_____

_____

What intentional actions will you take today to attract it?

1.

2.

3.

How will you feel while making these conscious efforts?

_____

_____

_____

I AM:

_____

_____

_____

EVENING RITUAL FOR   __ / __ /__

I AM:

_____

_____

_____

What three things are you grateful for today?

1.

2.

3.

How did you serve the universe today?

_____

_____

_____

How does it feel to experience your burning desire today?

_____

_____

_____

MORNING RITUAL FOR ___ / ___ /___

Your burning desire statement:

_____

_____

_____

What intentional actions will you take today to attract it?

1.

2.

3.

How will you feel while making these conscious efforts?

_____

_____

_____

I AM:

_____

_____

_____

EVENING RITUAL FOR ___ / ___ /___

I AM:

_____

_____

_____

What three things are you grateful for today?

1.

2.

3.

How did you serve the universe today?

_____

_____

_____

How does it feel to experience your burning desire today?

_____

_____

_____

MORNING RITUAL FOR   ___ / ___ /___

Your burning desire statement:

_____

_____

_____

What intentional actions will you take today to attract it?

1.

2.

3.

How will you feel while making these conscious efforts?

_____

_____

_____

I AM:

_____

_____

_____

EVENING RITUAL FOR   ___ / ___ /___

I AM:

_____

_____

_____

What three things are you grateful for today?

1.

2.

3.

How did you serve the universe today?

_____

_____

_____

How does it feel to experience your burning desire today?

_____

_____

_____

MORNING RITUAL FOR ___ / ___ / ___

Your burning desire statement:

_____

_____

_____

What intentional actions will you take today to attract it?

1.

2.

3.

How will you feel while making these conscious efforts?

_____

_____

_____

I AM:

_____

_____

_____

EVENING RITUAL FOR ___ / ___ / ___

I AM:

_____

_____

_____

What three things are you grateful for today?

1.

2.

3.

How did you serve the universe today?

_____

_____

_____

How does it feel to experience your burning desire today?

_____

_____

_____

MORNING RITUAL FOR ___ / ___ /___

Your burning desire statement:

_____

_____

_____

What intentional actions will you take today to attract it?

1.

2.

3.

How will you feel while making these conscious efforts?

_____

_____

_____

I AM:

_____

_____

_____

EVENING RITUAL FOR ___ / ___ /___

I AM:

_____

_____

_____

What three things are you grateful for today?

1.

2.

3.

How did you serve the universe today?

_____

_____

_____

How does it feel to experience your burning desire today?

_____

_____

_____

MORNING RITUAL FOR ___ / ___ /___

Your burning desire statement:

_____

_____

_____

What intentional actions will you take today to attract it?

1.

2.

3.

How will you feel while making these conscious efforts?

_____

_____

_____

I AM:

_____

_____

_____

EVENING RITUAL FOR   __ / __ /__

I AM:

_____

_____

_____

What three things are you grateful for today?

1.

2.

3.

How did you serve the universe today?

_____

_____

_____

How does it feel to experience your burning desire today?

_____

_____

_____

MORNING RITUAL FOR ___ / ___ /___

Your burning desire statement:

_____

_____

_____

What intentional actions will you take today to attract it?

1.

2.

3.

How will you feel while making these conscious efforts?

_____

_____

_____

I AM:

_____

_____

_____

EVENING RITUAL FOR ___ / ___ /___

I AM:

_____

_____

_____

What three things are you grateful for today?

1.

2.

3.

How did you serve the universe today?

_____

_____

_____

How does it feel to experience your burning desire today?

_____

_____

_____

MORNING RITUAL FOR ___ / ___ /___

Your burning desire statement:

_____

_____

_____

What intentional actions will you take today to attract it?

1.

2.

3.

How will you feel while making these conscious efforts?

_____

_____

_____

I AM:

_____

_____

_____

EVENING RITUAL FOR   ___ / ___ /___

I AM:

_____

_____

_____

What three things are you grateful for today?

1.

2.

3.

How did you serve the universe today?

_____

_____

_____

How does it feel to experience your burning desire today?

_____

_____

_____

MORNING RITUAL FOR ___ / ___ /___

Your burning desire statement:

_____

_____

_____

What intentional actions will you take today to attract it?

1.

2.

3.

How will you feel while making these conscious efforts?

_____

_____

_____

I AM:

_____

_____

_____

EVENING RITUAL FOR   ___ / ___ /___

I AM:

_____

_____

_____

What three things are you grateful for today?

1.

2.

3.

How did you serve the universe today?

_____

_____

_____

How does it feel to experience your burning desire today?

_____

_____

_____

MORNING RITUAL FOR ___ / ___ /___

Your burning desire statement:

_____

_____

_____

What intentional actions will you take today to attract it?

1.

2.

3.

How will you feel while making these conscious efforts?

_____

_____

_____

I AM:

_____

_____

_____

EVENING RITUAL FOR   ___ / ___ /___

I AM:

_____

_____

_____

What three things are you grateful for today?

1.

2.

3.

How did you serve the universe today?

_____

_____

_____

How does it feel to experience your burning desire today?

_____

_____

_____

MORNING RITUAL FOR ___ / ___ /___

Your burning desire statement:

_____

_____

_____

What intentional actions will you take today to attract it?

1.

2.

3.

How will you feel while making these conscious efforts?

_____

_____

_____

I AM:

_____

_____

_____

EVENING RITUAL FOR ___ / ___ / ___

I AM:

_____

_____

_____

What three things are you grateful for today?

1.

2.

3.

How did you serve the universe today?

_____

_____

_____

How does it feel to experience your burning desire today?

_____

_____

_____

MORNING RITUAL FOR ___ / ___ /___

Your burning desire statement:

_____

_____

_____

What intentional actions will you take today to attract it?

1.

2.

3.

How will you feel while making these conscious efforts?

_____

_____

_____

I AM:

_____

_____

_____

EVENING RITUAL FOR   __ / __ /__

I AM:

_____

_____

_____

What three things are you grateful for today?

1.

2.

3.

How did you serve the universe today?

_____

_____

_____

How does it feel to experience your burning desire today?

_____

_____

_____

MORNING RITUAL FOR ___ / ___ /___

Your burning desire statement:

_____

_____

_____

What intentional actions will you take today to attract it?

1.

2.

3.

How will you feel while making these conscious efforts?

_____

_____

_____

I AM:

_____

_____

_____

EVENING RITUAL FOR ___ / ___ /___

I AM:

_____

_____

_____

What three things are you grateful for today?

1.

2.

3.

How did you serve the universe today?

_____

_____

_____

How does it feel to experience your burning desire today?

_____

_____

_____

MORNING RITUAL FOR __ / __ /__

Your burning desire statement:

_____

_____

_____

What intentional actions will you take today to attract it?

1.

2.

3.

How will you feel while making these conscious efforts?

_____

_____

_____

I AM:

_____

_____

_____

EVENING RITUAL FOR   ___ / ___ /___

I AM:

_____

_____

_____

What three things are you grateful for today?

1.

2.

3.

How did you serve the universe today?

_____

_____

_____

How does it feel to experience your burning desire today?

_____

_____

_____

MORNING RITUAL FOR ___ / ___ /___

Your burning desire statement:

_____

_____

_____

What intentional actions will you take today to attract it?

1.

2.

3.

How will you feel while making these conscious efforts?

_____

_____

_____

I AM:

_____

_____

_____

EVENING RITUAL FOR   __ / __ /__

I AM:

_____

_____

_____

What three things are you grateful for today?

1.

2.

3.

How did you serve the universe today?

_____

_____

_____

How does it feel to experience your burning desire today?

_____

_____

_____

MORNING RITUAL FOR ___ / ___ /___

Your burning desire statement:

_____

_____

_____

What intentional actions will you take today to attract it?

1.

2.

3.

How will you feel while making these conscious efforts?

_____

_____

_____

I AM:

_____

_____

_____

EVENING RITUAL FOR ___ / ___ / ___

I AM:

_____

_____

_____

What three things are you grateful for today?

1.

2.

3.

How did you serve the universe today?

_____

_____

_____

How does it feel to experience your burning desire today?

_____

_____

_____

MORNING RITUAL FOR   __ / __ /__

Your burning desire statement:

_____

_____

_____

What intentional actions will you take today to attract it?

1.

2.

3.

How will you feel while making these conscious efforts?

_____

_____

_____

I AM:

_____

_____

_____

EVENING RITUAL FOR ___ / ___ /___

I AM:

_____

_____

_____

What three things are you grateful for today?

1.

2.

3.

How did you serve the universe today?

_____

_____

_____

How does it feel to experience your burning desire today?

_____

_____

_____

MORNING RITUAL FOR ___ / ___ /___

Your burning desire statement:

_____

_____

_____

What intentional actions will you take today to attract it?

1.

2.

3.

How will you feel while making these conscious efforts?

_____

_____

_____

I AM:

_____

_____

_____

EVENING RITUAL FOR ___ / ___ / ___

I AM:

_____

_____

_____

What three things are you grateful for today?

1.

2.

3.

How did you serve the universe today?

_____

_____

_____

How does it feel to experience your burning desire today?

_____

_____

_____

MORNING RITUAL FOR   ___ / ___ /___

Your burning desire statement:

_____

_____

_____

What intentional actions will you take today to attract it?

1.

2.

3.

How will you feel while making these conscious efforts?

_____

_____

_____

I AM:

_____

_____

_____

EVENING RITUAL FOR ___ / ___ /___

I AM:

_____

_____

_____

What three things are you grateful for today?

1.

2.

3.

How did you serve the universe today?

_____

_____

_____

How does it feel to experience your burning desire today?

_____

_____

_____

MORNING RITUAL FOR ___ / ___ / ___

Your burning desire statement:

_____

_____

_____

What intentional actions will you take today to attract it?

1.

2.

3.

How will you feel while making these conscious efforts?

_____

_____

_____

I AM:

_____

_____

_____

EVENING RITUAL FOR ___ / ___ /___

I AM:

_____

_____

_____

What three things are you grateful for today?

1.

2.

3.

How did you serve the universe today?

_____

_____

_____

How does it feel to experience your burning desire today?

_____

_____

_____

MORNING RITUAL FOR   __ / __ /__

Your burning desire statement:

_____

_____

_____

What intentional actions will you take today to attract it?

1.

2.

3.

How will you feel while making these conscious efforts?

_____

_____

_____

I AM:

_____

_____

_____

EVENING RITUAL FOR ___ / ___ /___

I AM:

_____

_____

_____

What three things are you grateful for today?

1.

2.

3.

How did you serve the universe today?

_____

_____

_____

How does it feel to experience your burning desire today?

_____

_____

_____

MORNING RITUAL FOR   __ / __ /__

Your burning desire statement:

_____

_____

_____

What intentional actions will you take today to attract it?

1.

2.

3.

How will you feel while making these conscious efforts?

_____

_____

_____

I AM:

_____

_____

_____

EVENING RITUAL FOR ___ / ___ /___

I AM:

_____

_____

_____

What three things are you grateful for today?

1.

2.

3.

How did you serve the universe today?

_____

_____

_____

How does it feel to experience your burning desire today?

_____

_____

_____

MORNING RITUAL FOR ___ / ___ /___

Your burning desire statement:

_____

_____

_____

What intentional actions will you take today to attract it?

1.

2.

3.

How will you feel while making these conscious efforts?

_____

_____

_____

I AM:

_____

_____

_____

EVENING RITUAL FOR ___ / ___ /___

I AM:

_____

_____

_____

What three things are you grateful for today?

1.

2.

3.

How did you serve the universe today?

_____

_____

_____

How does it feel to experience your burning desire today?

_____

_____

_____

MORNING RITUAL FOR ___ / ___ /___

Your burning desire statement:

_____

_____

_____

What intentional actions will you take today to attract it?

1.

2.

3.

How will you feel while making these conscious efforts?

_____

_____

_____

I AM:

_____

_____

_____

EVENING RITUAL FOR   ___ / ___ /___

I AM:

_____

_____

_____

What three things are you grateful for today?

1.

2.

3.

How did you serve the universe today?

_____

_____

_____

How does it feel to experience your burning desire today?

_____

_____

_____

MORNING RITUAL FOR ___ / ___ / ___

Your burning desire statement:

_____

_____

_____

What intentional actions will you take today to attract it?

1.

2.

3.

How will you feel while making these conscious efforts?

_____

_____

_____

I AM:

_____

_____

_____

EVENING RITUAL FOR   __ / __ / __

I AM:

_____

_____

_____

What three things are you grateful for today?

1.

2.

3.

How did you serve the universe today?

_____

_____

_____

How does it feel to experience your burning desire today?

_____

_____

_____

MORNING RITUAL FOR ___ / ___ /___

Your burning desire statement:

_____

_____

_____

What intentional actions will you take today to attract it?

1.

2.

3.

How will you feel while making these conscious efforts?

_____

_____

_____

I AM:

_____

_____

_____

EVENING RITUAL FOR ___ / ___ /___

I AM:

_____

_____

_____

What three things are you grateful for today?

1.

2.

3.

How did you serve the universe today?

_____

_____

_____

How does it feel to experience your burning desire today?

_____

_____

_____

MORNING RITUAL FOR ___ / ___ / ___

Your burning desire statement:

_____

_____

_____

What intentional actions will you take today to attract it?

1.

2.

3.

How will you feel while making these conscious efforts?

_____

_____

_____

I AM:

_____

_____

_____

EVENING RITUAL FOR ___ / ___ /___

I AM:

_____

_____

_____

What three things are you grateful for today?

1.

2.

3.

How did you serve the universe today?

_____

_____

_____

How does it feel to experience your burning desire today?

_____

_____

_____

MORNING RITUAL FOR ___ / ___ / ___

Your burning desire statement:

_____

_____

_____

What intentional actions will you take today to attract it?

1.

2.

3.

How will you feel while making these conscious efforts?

_____

_____

_____

I AM:

_____

_____

_____

EVENING RITUAL FOR ___ / ___ /___

I AM:

_____

_____

_____

What three things are you grateful for today?

1.

2.

3.

How did you serve the universe today?

_____

_____

_____

How does it feel to experience your burning desire today?

_____

_____

_____

MORNING RITUAL FOR ___ / ___ /___

Your burning desire statement:

_____

_____

_____

What intentional actions will you take today to attract it?

1.

2.

3.

How will you feel while making these conscious efforts?

_____

_____

_____

I AM:

_____

_____

_____

EVENING RITUAL FOR   __ / __ /__

I AM:

_____

_____

_____

What three things are you grateful for today?

1.

2.

3.

How did you serve the universe today?

_____

_____

_____

How does it feel to experience your burning desire today?

_____

_____

_____

MORNING RITUAL FOR ___ / ___ / ___

Your burning desire statement:

_____

_____

_____

What intentional actions will you take today to attract it?

1.

2.

3.

How will you feel while making these conscious efforts?

_____

_____

_____

I AM:

_____

_____

_____

EVENING RITUAL FOR ___ / ___ / ___

I AM:

_____

_____

_____

What three things are you grateful for today?

1.

2.

3.

How did you serve the universe today?

_____

_____

_____

How does it feel to experience your burning desire today?

_____

_____

_____

MORNING RITUAL FOR ___ / ___ /___

Your burning desire statement:

_____

_____

_____

What intentional actions will you take today to attract it?

1.

2.

3.

How will you feel while making these conscious efforts?

_____

_____

_____

I AM:

_____

_____

_____

EVENING RITUAL FOR ___ / ___ / ___

I AM:

_____

_____

_____

What three things are you grateful for today?

1.

2.

3.

How did you serve the universe today?

_____

_____

_____

How does it feel to experience your burning desire today?

_____

_____

_____

MORNING RITUAL FOR ___ / ___ /___

Your burning desire statement:

_____

_____

_____

What intentional actions will you take today to attract it?

1.

2.

3.

How will you feel while making these conscious efforts?

_____

_____

_____

I AM:

_____

_____

_____

EVENING RITUAL FOR   ___ / ___ /___

I AM:

_____

_____

_____

What three things are you grateful for today?

1.

2.

3.

How did you serve the universe today?

_____

_____

_____

How does it feel to experience your burning desire today?

_____

_____

_____

MORNING RITUAL FOR ___ / ___ /___

Your burning desire statement:

_____

_____

_____

What intentional actions will you take today to attract it?

1.

2.

3.

How will you feel while making these conscious efforts?

_____

_____

_____

I AM:

_____

_____

_____

EVENING RITUAL FOR   __ / __ /__

I AM:

_____

_____

_____

What three things are you grateful for today?

1.

2.

3.

How did you serve the universe today?

_____

_____

_____

How does it feel to experience your burning desire today?

_____

_____

_____

MORNING RITUAL FOR ___ / ___ /___

Your burning desire statement:

_____

_____

_____

What intentional actions will you take today to attract it?

1.

2.

3.

How will you feel while making these conscious efforts?

_____

_____

_____

I AM:

_____

_____

_____

EVENING RITUAL FOR   __ / __ /__

I AM:

_____

_____

_____

What three things are you grateful for today?

1.

2.

3.

How did you serve the universe today?

_____

_____

_____

How does it feel to experience your burning desire today?

_____

_____

_____

MORNING RITUAL FOR ___ / ___ /___

Your burning desire statement:

_____

_____

_____

What intentional actions will you take today to attract it?

1.

2.

3.

How will you feel while making these conscious efforts?

_____

_____

_____

I AM:

_____

_____

_____

EVENING RITUAL FOR ___ / ___ /___

I AM:

_____

_____

_____

What three things are you grateful for today?

1.

2.

3.

How did you serve the universe today?

_____

_____

_____

How does it feel to experience your burning desire today?

_____

_____

_____

MORNING RITUAL FOR ___ / ___ /___

Your burning desire statement:

_____

_____

_____

What intentional actions will you take today to attract it?

1.

2.

3.

How will you feel while making these conscious efforts?

_____

_____

_____

I AM:

_____

_____

_____

EVENING RITUAL FOR   __ / __ /__

I AM:

_____

_____

_____

What three things are you grateful for today?

1.

2.

3.

How did you serve the universe today?

_____

_____

_____

How does it feel to experience your burning desire today?

_____

_____

_____

MORNING RITUAL FOR ___ / ___ /___

Your burning desire statement:

_____

_____

_____

What intentional actions will you take today to attract it?

1.

2.

3.

How will you feel while making these conscious efforts?

_____

_____

_____

I AM:

_____

_____

_____

EVENING RITUAL FOR   __ / __ /__

I AM:

_____

_____

_____

What three things are you grateful for today?

1.

2.

3.

How did you serve the universe today?

_____

_____

_____

How does it feel to experience your burning desire today?

_____

_____

_____

MORNING RITUAL FOR ___ / ___ /___

Your burning desire statement:

_____

_____

_____

What intentional actions will you take today to attract it?

1.

2.

3.

How will you feel while making these conscious efforts?

_____

_____

_____

I AM:

_____

_____

_____

EVENING RITUAL FOR   __ / __ /__

I AM:

_____

_____

_____

What three things are you grateful for today?

1.

2.

3.

How did you serve the universe today?

_____

_____

_____

How does it feel to experience your burning desire today?

_____

_____

_____

MORNING RITUAL FOR ___ / ___ /___

Your burning desire statement:

_____

_____

_____

What intentional actions will you take today to attract it?

1.

2.

3.

How will you feel while making these conscious efforts?

_____

_____

_____

I AM:

_____

_____

_____

EVENING RITUAL FOR ___ / ___ / ___

I AM:

_____

_____

_____

What three things are you grateful for today?

1.

2.

3.

How did you serve the universe today?

_____

_____

_____

How does it feel to experience your burning desire today?

_____

_____

_____

MORNING RITUAL FOR ___ / ___ / ___

Your burning desire statement:

_____

_____

_____

What intentional actions will you take today to attract it?

1.

2.

3.

How will you feel while making these conscious efforts?

_____

_____

_____

I AM:

_____

_____

_____

EVENING RITUAL FOR   __ / __ /__

I AM:

_____

_____

_____

What three things are you grateful for today?

1.

2.

3.

How did you serve the universe today?

_____

_____

_____

How does it feel to experience your burning desire today?

_____

_____

_____

MORNING RITUAL FOR ___ / ___ /___

Your burning desire statement:

_____

_____

_____

What intentional actions will you take today to attract it?

1.

2.

3.

How will you feel while making these conscious efforts?

_____

_____

_____

I AM:

_____

_____

_____

EVENING RITUAL FOR ___ / ___ /___

I AM:

_____

_____

_____

What three things are you grateful for today?

1.

2.

3.

How did you serve the universe today?

_____

_____

_____

How does it feel to experience your burning desire today?

_____

_____

_____

MORNING RITUAL FOR   __ / __ /__

Your burning desire statement:

_____

_____

_____

What intentional actions will you take today to attract it?

1.

2.

3.

How will you feel while making these conscious efforts?

_____

_____

_____

I AM:

_____

_____

_____

EVENING RITUAL FOR ___ / ___ /___

I AM:

_____

_____

_____

What three things are you grateful for today?

1.

2.

3.

How did you serve the universe today?

_____

_____

_____

How does it feel to experience your burning desire today?

_____

_____

_____

MORNING RITUAL FOR ___ / ___ /___

Your burning desire statement:

_____

_____

_____

What intentional actions will you take today to attract it?

1.

2.

3.

How will you feel while making these conscious efforts?

_____

_____

_____

I AM:

_____

_____

_____

EVENING RITUAL FOR ___ / ___ / ___

I AM:

_____

_____

_____

What three things are you grateful for today?

1.

2.

3.

How did you serve the universe today?

_____

_____

_____

How does it feel to experience your burning desire today?

_____

_____

_____

MORNING RITUAL FOR   ___ / ___ /___

Your burning desire statement:

_____

_____

_____

What intentional actions will you take today to attract it?

1.

2.

3.

How will you feel while making these conscious efforts?

_____

_____

_____

I AM:

_____

_____

_____

EVENING RITUAL FOR   ___ / ___ /___

I AM:

_____

_____

_____

What three things are you grateful for today?

1.

2.

3.

How did you serve the universe today?

_____

_____

_____

How does it feel to experience your burning desire today?

_____

_____

_____

MORNING RITUAL FOR ___ / ___ / ___

Your burning desire statement:

_____

_____

_____

What intentional actions will you take today to attract it?

1.

2.

3.

How will you feel while making these conscious efforts?

_____

_____

_____

I AM:

_____

_____

_____

EVENING RITUAL FOR ___ / ___ /___

I AM:

_____

_____

_____

What three things are you grateful for today?

1.

2.

3.

How did you serve the universe today?

_____

_____

_____

How does it feel to experience your burning desire today?

_____

_____

_____

MORNING RITUAL FOR   __ / __ /__

Your burning desire statement:

_____

_____

_____

What intentional actions will you take today to attract it?

1.

2.

3.

How will you feel while making these conscious efforts?

_____

_____

_____

I AM:

_____

_____

_____

EVENING RITUAL FOR   __ / __ /__

I AM:

_____

_____

_____

What three things are you grateful for today?

1.

2.

3.

How did you serve the universe today?

_____

_____

_____

How does it feel to experience your burning desire today?

_____

_____

_____

THE I AM JOURNAL

MORNING RITUAL FOR ___ / ___ / ___

Your burning desire statement:

_____

_____

_____

What intentional actions will you take today to attract it?

1.

2.

3.

How will you feel while making these conscious efforts?

_____

_____

_____

I AM:

_____

_____

_____

EVENING RITUAL FOR ___ / ___ /___

I AM:

_____

_____

_____

What three things are you grateful for today?

1.

2.

3.

How did you serve the universe today?

_____

_____

_____

How does it feel to experience your burning desire today?

_____

_____

_____

MORNING RITUAL FOR   __ / __ /__

Your burning desire statement:

_____

_____

_____

What intentional actions will you take today to attract it?

1.

2.

3.

How will you feel while making these conscious efforts?

_____

_____

_____

I AM:

_____

_____

_____

EVENING RITUAL FOR ___ / ___ /___

I AM:

_____

_____

_____

What three things are you grateful for today?

1.

2.

3.

How did you serve the universe today?

_____

_____

_____

How does it feel to experience your burning desire today?

_____

_____

_____

MORNING RITUAL FOR ___ / ___ /___

Your burning desire statement:

_____

_____

_____

What intentional actions will you take today to attract it?

1.

2.

3.

How will you feel while making these conscious efforts?

_____

_____

_____

I AM:

_____

_____

_____

EVENING RITUAL FOR ___ / ___ /___

I AM:

_____

_____

_____

What three things are you grateful for today?

1.

2.

3.

How did you serve the universe today?

_____

_____

_____

How does it feel to experience your burning desire today?

_____

_____

_____

MORNING RITUAL FOR ___ / ___ /___

Your burning desire statement:

_____

_____

_____

What intentional actions will you take today to attract it?

1.

2.

3.

How will you feel while making these conscious efforts?

_____

_____

_____

I AM:

_____

_____

_____

EVENING RITUAL FOR ___ / ___ /___

I AM:

_____

_____

_____

What three things are you grateful for today?

1.

2.

3.

How did you serve the universe today?

_____

_____

_____

How does it feel to experience your burning desire today?

_____

_____

_____

MORNING RITUAL FOR ___ / ___ /___

Your burning desire statement:

_____

_____

_____

What intentional actions will you take today to attract it?

1.

2.

3.

How will you feel while making these conscious efforts?

_____

_____

_____

I AM:

_____

_____

_____

EVENING RITUAL FOR   __ / __ /__

I AM:

_____

_____

_____

What three things are you grateful for today?

1.

2.

3.

How did you serve the universe today?

_____

_____

_____

How does it feel to experience your burning desire today?

_____

_____

_____

MORNING RITUAL FOR ___ / ___ /___

Your burning desire statement:

_____

_____

_____

What intentional actions will you take today to attract it?

1.

2.

3.

How will you feel while making these conscious efforts?

_____

_____

_____

I AM:

_____

_____

_____

EVENING RITUAL FOR   __ / __ /__

I AM:

_____

_____

_____

What three things are you grateful for today?

1.

2.

3.

How did you serve the universe today?

_____

_____

_____

How does it feel to experience your burning desire today?

_____

_____

_____

MORNING RITUAL FOR ___ / ___ /___

Your burning desire statement:

_____

_____

_____

What intentional actions will you take today to attract it?

1.

2.

3.

How will you feel while making these conscious efforts?

_____

_____

_____

I AM:

_____

_____

_____

EVENING RITUAL FOR   __ / __ /__

I AM:

_____

_____

_____

What three things are you grateful for today?

1.

2.

3.

How did you serve the universe today?

_____

_____

_____

How does it feel to experience your burning desire today?

_____

_____

_____

MORNING RITUAL FOR ___ / ___ /___

Your burning desire statement:

_____

_____

_____

What intentional actions will you take today to attract it?

1.

2.

3.

How will you feel while making these conscious efforts?

_____

_____

_____

I AM:

_____

_____

_____

EVENING RITUAL FOR ___ / ___ /___

I AM:

_____

_____

_____

What three things are you grateful for today?

1.

2.

3.

How did you serve the universe today?

_____

_____

_____

How does it feel to experience your burning desire today?

_____

_____

_____

MORNING RITUAL FOR ___ / ___ /___

Your burning desire statement:

_____

_____

_____

What intentional actions will you take today to attract it?

1.

2.

3.

How will you feel while making these conscious efforts?

_____

_____

_____

I AM:

_____

_____

_____

EVENING RITUAL FOR ___ / ___ /___

I AM:

_____

_____

_____

What three things are you grateful for today?

1.

2.

3.

How did you serve the universe today?

_____

_____

_____

How does it feel to experience your burning desire today?

_____

_____

_____

MORNING RITUAL FOR ___ / ___ /___

Your burning desire statement:

_____

_____

_____

What intentional actions will you take today to attract it?

1.

2.

3.

How will you feel while making these conscious efforts?

_____

_____

_____

I AM:

_____

_____

_____

EVENING RITUAL FOR __ / __ / __

I AM:

_____

_____

_____

What three things are you grateful for today?

1.

2.

3.

How did you serve the universe today?

_____

_____

_____

How does it feel to experience your burning desire today?

_____

_____

_____

MORNING RITUAL FOR ___ / ___ /___

Your burning desire statement:

_____

_____

_____

What intentional actions will you take today to attract it?

1.

2.

3.

How will you feel while making these conscious efforts?

_____

_____

_____

I AM:

_____

_____

_____

EVENING RITUAL FOR   __ / __ /__

I AM:

_____

_____

_____

What three things are you grateful for today?

1.

2.

3.

How did you serve the universe today?

_____

_____

_____

How does it feel to experience your burning desire today?

_____

_____

_____

MORNING RITUAL FOR ___ / ___ /___

Your burning desire statement:

_____

_____

_____

What intentional actions will you take today to attract it?

1.

2.

3.

How will you feel while making these conscious efforts?

_____

_____

_____

I AM:

_____

_____

_____

EVENING RITUAL FOR   __ / __ /__

I AM:

_____

_____

_____

What three things are you grateful for today?

1.

2.

3.

How did you serve the universe today?

_____

_____

_____

How does it feel to experience your burning desire today?

_____

_____

_____

MORNING RITUAL FOR ___ / ___ /___

Your burning desire statement:

_____

_____

_____

What intentional actions will you take today to attract it?

1.

2.

3.

How will you feel while making these conscious efforts?

_____

_____

_____

I AM:

_____

_____

_____

EVENING RITUAL FOR ___ / ___ / ___

I AM:

_____

_____

_____

What three things are you grateful for today?

1.

2.

3.

How did you serve the universe today?

_____

_____

_____

How does it feel to experience your burning desire today?

_____

_____

_____

MORNING RITUAL FOR ___ / ___ / ___

Your burning desire statement:

_____

_____

_____

What intentional actions will you take today to attract it?

1.

2.

3.

How will you feel while making these conscious efforts?

_____

_____

_____

I AM:

_____

_____

_____

EVENING RITUAL FOR   ___ / ___ /___

I AM:

_____

_____

_____

What three things are you grateful for today?

1.

2.

3.

How did you serve the universe today?

_____

_____

_____

How does it feel to experience your burning desire today?

_____

_____

_____

MORNING RITUAL FOR ___ / ___ /___

Your burning desire statement:

_____

_____

_____

What intentional actions will you take today to attract it?

1.

2.

3.

How will you feel while making these conscious efforts?

_____

_____

_____

I AM:

_____

_____

_____

EVENING RITUAL FOR ___ / ___ /___

I AM:

_____

_____

_____

What three things are you grateful for today?

1.

2.

3.

How did you serve the universe today?

_____

_____

_____

How does it feel to experience your burning desire today?

_____

_____

_____

MORNING RITUAL FOR   __ / __ /__

Your burning desire statement:

_____

_____

_____

What intentional actions will you take today to attract it?

1.

2.

3.

How will you feel while making these conscious efforts?

_____

_____

_____

I AM:

_____

_____

_____

EVENING RITUAL FOR ___ / ___ /___

I AM:

_____

_____

_____

What three things are you grateful for today?

1.

2.

3.

How did you serve the universe today?

_____

_____

_____

How does it feel to experience your burning desire today?

_____

_____

_____

MORNING RITUAL FOR ___ / ___ /___

Your burning desire statement:

_____

_____

_____

What intentional actions will you take today to attract it?

1.

2.

3.

How will you feel while making these conscious efforts?

_____

_____

_____

I AM:

_____

_____

_____

EVENING RITUAL FOR   ___ / ___ /___

I AM:

_____

_____

_____

What three things are you grateful for today?

1.

2.

3.

How did you serve the universe today?

_____

_____

_____

How does it feel to experience your burning desire today?

_____

_____

_____

MORNING RITUAL FOR ___ / ___ /___

Your burning desire statement:

_____

_____

_____

What intentional actions will you take today to attract it?

1.

2.

3.

How will you feel while making these conscious efforts?

_____

_____

_____

I AM:

_____

_____

_____

EVENING RITUAL FOR ___ / ___ /___

I AM:

_____

_____

_____

What three things are you grateful for today?

1.

2.

3.

How did you serve the universe today?

_____

_____

_____

How does it feel to experience your burning desire today?

_____

_____

_____

MORNING RITUAL FOR ___ / ___ /___

Your burning desire statement:

_____

_____

_____

What intentional actions will you take today to attract it?

1.

2.

3.

How will you feel while making these conscious efforts?

_____

_____

_____

I AM:

_____

_____

_____

EVENING RITUAL FOR ___ / ___ / ___

I AM:

_____

_____

_____

What three things are you grateful for today?

1.

2.

3.

How did you serve the universe today?

_____

_____

_____

How does it feel to experience your burning desire today?

_____

_____

_____

MORNING RITUAL FOR ___ / ___ / ___

Your burning desire statement:

_____

_____

_____

What intentional actions will you take today to attract it?

1.

2.

3.

How will you feel while making these conscious efforts?

_____

_____

_____

I AM:

_____

_____

_____

EVENING RITUAL FOR   __ / __ / __

I AM:

_____

_____

_____

What three things are you grateful for today?

1.

2.

3.

How did you serve the universe today?

_____

_____

_____

How does it feel to experience your burning desire today?

_____

_____

_____

MORNING RITUAL FOR ___ / ___ /___

Your burning desire statement:

_____

_____

_____

What intentional actions will you take today to attract it?

1.

2.

3.

How will you feel while making these conscious efforts?

_____

_____

_____

I AM:

_____

_____

_____

EVENING RITUAL FOR ___ / ___ /___

I AM:

_____

_____

_____

What three things are you grateful for today?

1.

2.

3.

How did you serve the universe today?

_____

_____

_____

How does it feel to experience your burning desire today?

_____

_____

_____

MORNING RITUAL FOR ___ / ___ /___

Your burning desire statement:

_____

_____

_____

What intentional actions will you take today to attract it?

1.

2.

3.

How will you feel while making these conscious efforts?

_____

_____

_____

I AM:

_____

_____

_____

EVENING RITUAL FOR ___ / ___ /___

I AM:

_____

_____

_____

What three things are you grateful for today?

1.

2.

3.

How did you serve the universe today?

_____

_____

_____

How does it feel to experience your burning desire today?

_____

_____

_____

MORNING RITUAL FOR ___ / ___ /___

Your burning desire statement:

_____

_____

_____

What intentional actions will you take today to attract it?

1.

2.

3.

How will you feel while making these conscious efforts?

_____

_____

_____

I AM:

_____

_____

_____

EVENING RITUAL FOR   ___ / ___ /___

I AM:

_____

_____

_____

What three things are you grateful for today?

1.

2.

3.

How did you serve the universe today?

_____

_____

_____

How does it feel to experience your burning desire today?

_____

_____

_____

MORNING RITUAL FOR ___ / ___ /___

Your burning desire statement:

_____

_____

_____

What intentional actions will you take today to attract it?

1.

2.

3.

How will you feel while making these conscious efforts?

_____

_____

_____

I AM:

_____

_____

_____

EVENING RITUAL FOR   __ / __ /__

I AM:

_____

_____

_____

What three things are you grateful for today?

1.

2.

3.

How did you serve the universe today?

_____

_____

_____

How does it feel to experience your burning desire today?

_____

_____

_____

MORNING RITUAL FOR ___ / ___ / ___

Your burning desire statement:

_____

_____

_____

What intentional actions will you take today to attract it?

1.

2.

3.

How will you feel while making these conscious efforts?

_____

_____

_____

I AM:

_____

_____

_____

EVENING RITUAL FOR   ___ / ___ /___

I AM:

_____

_____

_____

What three things are you grateful for today?

1.

2.

3.

How did you serve the universe today?

_____

_____

_____

How does it feel to experience your burning desire today?

_____

_____

_____

MORNING RITUAL FOR ___ / ___ /___

Your burning desire statement:

_____

_____

_____

What intentional actions will you take today to attract it?

1.

2.

3.

How will you feel while making these conscious efforts?

_____

_____

_____

I AM:

_____

_____

_____

EVENING RITUAL FOR ___ / ___ /___

I AM:

_____

_____

_____

What three things are you grateful for today?

1.

2.

3.

How did you serve the universe today?

_____

_____

_____

How does it feel to experience your burning desire today?

_____

_____

_____

MORNING RITUAL FOR ___ / ___ / ___

Your burning desire statement:

_____

_____

_____

What intentional actions will you take today to attract it?

1.

2.

3.

How will you feel while making these conscious efforts?

_____

_____

_____

I AM:

_____

_____

_____

EVENING RITUAL FOR   __ / __ /__

I AM:

_____

_____

_____

What three things are you grateful for today?

1.

2.

3.

How did you serve the universe today?

_____

_____

_____

How does it feel to experience your burning desire today?

_____

_____

_____

MORNING RITUAL FOR __ / __ /__

Your burning desire statement:

_____

_____

_____

What intentional actions will you take today to attract it?

1.

2.

3.

How will you feel while making these conscious efforts?

_____

_____

_____

I AM:

_____

_____

_____

EVENING RITUAL FOR ___ / ___ /___

I AM:

_____

_____

_____

What three things are you grateful for today?

1.

2.

3.

How did you serve the universe today?

_____

_____

_____

How does it feel to experience your burning desire today?

_____

_____

_____

MORNING RITUAL FOR __ / __ /__

Your burning desire statement:

_____

_____

_____

What intentional actions will you take today to attract it?

1.

2.

3.

How will you feel while making these conscious efforts?

_____

_____

_____

I AM:

_____

_____

_____

EVENING RITUAL FOR ___ / ___ /___

I AM:

_____

_____

_____

What three things are you grateful for today?

1.

2.

3.

How did you serve the universe today?

_____

_____

_____

How does it feel to experience your burning desire today?

_____

_____

_____

MORNING RITUAL FOR ___ / ___ /___

Your burning desire statement:

_____

_____

_____

What intentional actions will you take today to attract it?

1.

2.

3.

How will you feel while making these conscious efforts?

_____

_____

_____

I AM:

_____

_____

_____

EVENING RITUAL FOR ___ / ___ /___

I AM:

_____

_____

_____

What three things are you grateful for today?

1.

2.

3.

How did you serve the universe today?

_____

_____

_____

How does it feel to experience your burning desire today?

_____

_____

_____

MORNING RITUAL FOR ___ / ___ / ___

Your burning desire statement:

_____

_____

_____

What intentional actions will you take today to attract it?

1.

2.

3.

How will you feel while making these conscious efforts?

_____

_____

_____

I AM:

_____

_____

_____

EVENING RITUAL FOR   __ / __ /__

I AM:

_____

_____

_____

What three things are you grateful for today?

1.

2.

3.

How did you serve the universe today?

_____

_____

_____

How does it feel to experience your burning desire today?

_____

_____

_____

MORNING RITUAL FOR   __ / __ /__

Your burning desire statement:

_____

_____

_____

What intentional actions will you take today to attract it?

1.

2.

3.

How will you feel while making these conscious efforts?

_____

_____

_____

I AM:

_____

_____

_____

EVENING RITUAL FOR   __ / __ /__

I AM:

_____

_____

_____

What three things are you grateful for today?

1.

2.

3.

How did you serve the universe today?

_____

_____

_____

How does it feel to experience your burning desire today?

_____

_____

_____

MORNING RITUAL FOR ___ / ___ /___

Your burning desire statement:

_____

_____

_____

What intentional actions will you take today to attract it?

1.

2.

3.

How will you feel while making these conscious efforts?

_____

_____

_____

I AM:

_____

_____

_____

EVENING RITUAL FOR ___ / ___ /___

I AM:

_____

_____

_____

What three things are you grateful for today?

1.

2.

3.

How did you serve the universe today?

_____

_____

_____

How does it feel to experience your burning desire today?

_____

_____

_____

MORNING RITUAL FOR   __ / __ /__

Your burning desire statement:

_____

_____

_____

What intentional actions will you take today to attract it?

1.

2.

3.

How will you feel while making these conscious efforts?

_____

_____

_____

I AM:

_____

_____

_____

EVENING RITUAL FOR   ___ / ___ /___

I AM:

_____

_____

_____

What three things are you grateful for today?

1.

2.

3.

How did you serve the universe today?

_____

_____

_____

How does it feel to experience your burning desire today?

_____

_____

_____

MORNING RITUAL FOR __ / __ /__

Your burning desire statement:

_____

_____

_____

What intentional actions will you take today to attract it?

1.

2.

3.

How will you feel while making these conscious efforts?

_____

_____

_____

I AM:

_____

_____

_____

EVENING RITUAL FOR   ___ / ___ /___

I AM:

_____

_____

_____

What three things are you grateful for today?

1.

2.

3.

How did you serve the universe today?

_____

_____

_____

How does it feel to experience your burning desire today?

_____

_____

_____

MORNING RITUAL FOR ___ / ___ /___

Your burning desire statement:

_____

_____

_____

What intentional actions will you take today to attract it?

1.

2.

3.

How will you feel while making these conscious efforts?

_____

_____

_____

I AM:

_____

_____

_____

EVENING RITUAL FOR   __ / __ /__

I AM:

_____

_____

_____

What three things are you grateful for today?

1.

2.

3.

How did you serve the universe today?

_____

_____

How does it feel to experience your burning desire today?

_____

_____

_____

MORNING RITUAL FOR ___ / ___ /___

Your burning desire statement:

_____

_____

_____

What intentional actions will you take today to attract it?

1.

2.

3.

How will you feel while making these conscious efforts?

_____

_____

_____

I AM:

_____

_____

_____

EVENING RITUAL FOR ___ / ___ / ___

I AM:

_____

_____

_____

What three things are you grateful for today?

1.

2.

3.

How did you serve the universe today?

_____

_____

_____

How does it feel to experience your burning desire today?

_____

_____

_____

MORNING RITUAL FOR ___ / ___ /___

Your burning desire statement:

_____

_____

_____

What intentional actions will you take today to attract it?

1.

2.

3.

How will you feel while making these conscious efforts?

_____

_____

_____

I AM:

_____

_____

_____

EVENING RITUAL FOR   __ / __ /__

I AM:

_____

_____

_____

What three things are you grateful for today?

1.

2.

3.

How did you serve the universe today?

_____

_____

_____

How does it feel to experience your burning desire today?

_____

_____

_____

MORNING RITUAL FOR   __ / __ /__

Your burning desire statement:

_____

_____

_____

What intentional actions will you take today to attract it?

1.

2.

3.

How will you feel while making these conscious efforts?

_____

_____

_____

I AM:

_____

_____

_____

EVENING RITUAL FOR   ___ / ___ /___

I AM:

_____

_____

_____

What three things are you grateful for today?

1.

2.

3.

How did you serve the universe today?

_____

_____

_____

How does it feel to experience your burning desire today?

_____

_____

_____

MORNING RITUAL FOR __ / __ /__

Your burning desire statement:

_____

_____

_____

What intentional actions will you take today to attract it?

1.

2.

3.

How will you feel while making these conscious efforts?

_____

_____

_____

I AM:

_____

_____

_____

EVENING RITUAL FOR   __ / __ / __

I AM:

_____

_____

_____

What three things are you grateful for today?

1.

2.

3.

How did you serve the universe today?

_____

_____

_____

How does it feel to experience your burning desire today?

_____

_____

_____

MORNING RITUAL FOR ___ / ___ /___

Your burning desire statement:

_____

_____

_____

What intentional actions will you take today to attract it?

1.

2.

3.

How will you feel while making these conscious efforts?

_____

_____

_____

I AM:

_____

_____

_____

EVENING RITUAL FOR   __ / __ /__

I AM:

_____

_____

_____

What three things are you grateful for today?

1.

2.

3.

How did you serve the universe today?

_____

_____

_____

How does it feel to experience your burning desire today?

_____

_____

_____

MORNING RITUAL FOR ___ / ___ /___

Your burning desire statement:

_____

_____

_____

What intentional actions will you take today to attract it?

1.

2.

3.

How will you feel while making these conscious efforts?

_____

_____

_____

I AM:

_____

_____

_____

EVENING RITUAL FOR ___ / ___ /___

I AM:

_____

_____

_____

What three things are you grateful for today?

1.

2.

3.

How did you serve the universe today?

_____

_____

_____

How does it feel to experience your burning desire today?

_____

_____

_____

MORNING RITUAL FOR ___ / ___ / ___

Your burning desire statement:

_____

_____

_____

What intentional actions will you take today to attract it?

1.

2.

3.

How will you feel while making these conscious efforts?

_____

_____

_____

I AM:

_____

_____

_____

EVENING RITUAL FOR   __ / __ /__

I AM:

_____

_____

_____

What three things are you grateful for today?

1.

2.

3.

How did you serve the universe today?

_____

_____

_____

How does it feel to experience your burning desire today?

_____

_____

_____

MORNING RITUAL FOR ___ / ___ /___

Your burning desire statement:

_____

_____

_____

What intentional actions will you take today to attract it?

1.

2.

3.

How will you feel while making these conscious efforts?

_____

_____

_____

I AM:

_____

_____

_____

EVENING RITUAL FOR ___ / ___ /___

I AM:

_____

_____

_____

What three things are you grateful for today?

1.

2.

3.

How did you serve the universe today?

_____

_____

_____

How does it feel to experience your burning desire today?

_____

_____

_____

MORNING RITUAL FOR ___ / ___ /___

Your burning desire statement:

_____

_____

_____

What intentional actions will you take today to attract it?

1.

2.

3.

How will you feel while making these conscious efforts?

_____

_____

_____

I AM:

_____

_____

_____

EVENING RITUAL FOR   __ / __ /__

I AM:

_____

_____

_____

What three things are you grateful for today?

1.

2.

3.

How did you serve the universe today?

_____

_____

_____

How does it feel to experience your burning desire today?

_____

_____

_____

MORNING RITUAL FOR ___ / ___ /___

Your burning desire statement:

_____

_____

_____

What intentional actions will you take today to attract it?

1.

2.

3.

How will you feel while making these conscious efforts?

_____

_____

_____

I AM:

_____

_____

_____

EVENING RITUAL FOR   __ / __ /__

I AM:

_____

_____

_____

What three things are you grateful for today?

1.

2.

3.

How did you serve the universe today?

_____

_____

_____

How does it feel to experience your burning desire today?

_____

_____

_____

MORNING RITUAL FOR ___ / ___ / ___

Your burning desire statement:

_____

_____

_____

What intentional actions will you take today to attract it?

1.

2.

3.

How will you feel while making these conscious efforts?

_____

_____

_____

I AM:

_____

_____

_____

EVENING RITUAL FOR ___ / ___ /___

I AM:

_____

_____

_____

What three things are you grateful for today?

1.

2.

3.

How did you serve the universe today?

_____

_____

_____

How does it feel to experience your burning desire today?

_____

_____

_____

MORNING RITUAL FOR ___ / ___ /___

Your burning desire statement:

_____

_____

_____

What intentional actions will you take today to attract it?

1.

2.

3.

How will you feel while making these conscious efforts?

_____

_____

_____

I AM:

_____

_____

_____

EVENING RITUAL FOR ___ / ___ /___

I AM:

_____

_____

_____

What three things are you grateful for today?

1.

2.

3.

How did you serve the universe today?

_____

_____

_____

How does it feel to experience your burning desire today?

_____

_____

_____

YOU DID IT.

Congratulations on taking this journey to spiritually manifest your dream life. Along the way you've probably faced doubts, questioned the process and become impatient.

That's normal.

But what sets you apart from many others is that you took action. You raised your vibration. You changed your feelings. You are changing your world, but you may not realize it yet. Have faith in the process and stay on this path to spiritually manifest a life full of joy, success and abundance.

We'd love to hear how The I AM Journal has helped you put the Law of Attraction into action. Please share your stories with us at hello@thinkandinkco.com.